Listening to Young Children
in Early Years Settings

by the same author

Promoting Young Children's Emotional Health and Wellbeing
A Practical Guide for Professionals and Parents
Sonia Mainstone-Cotton
ISBN 978 1 78592 054 7
eISBN 978 1 78450 311 6

Promoting Emotional Wellbeing in Early Years Staff
A Practical Guide for Looking after Yourself and Your Colleagues
Sonia Mainstone-Cotton
ISBN 978 1 78592 335 7
eISBN 978 1 78450 656 8

Can I tell you about Bipolar Disorder?
A guide for friends, family and professionals
Sonia Mainstone-Cotton
Illustrated by Jon Birch
ISBN 978 1 78592 470 5
eISBN 978 1 78450 854 8
Part of the *Can I tell you about...?* series

of related interest

Giving Children a Voice
A Step-by-Step Guide to Promoting Child-Centred Practice
Sam Frankel
ISBN 978 1 78592 278 7
eISBN 978 1 78450 578 3

Listening to Young Children
A Guide to Understanding and Using the Mosaic Approach
Expanded Third Edition
Alison Clark
Foreword by Peter Moss
ISBN 978 1 90939 122 2
eISBN 978 1 90939 126 0

Supporting Toddlers' Wellbeing in Early Years Settings
Strategies and Tools for Practitioners and Teachers
Edited by Helen Sutherland and Yasmin Mukadam
ISBN 978 1 78592 262 6
eISBN 978 1 78450 552 3

Listening to Young Children in Early Years Settings

A Practical Guide

Sonia Mainstone-Cotton

Jessica Kingsley *Publishers*
London and Philadelphia

First published in 2019
by Jessica Kingsley Publishers
73 Collier Street
London N1 9BE, UK
and
400 Market Street, Suite 400
Philadelphia, PA 19106, USA

www.jkp.com

Library of Congress Cataloging in Publication Data
Names: Mainstone-Cotton, Sonia, author.
Title: Listening to young children in early years settings : a practical
  guide / Sonia Mainstone-Cotton.
Description: London ; Philadelphia : Jessica Kingsley Publishers, 2019. |
  Includes bibliographical references and index.
Identifiers: LCCN 2018012621 | ISBN 9781785924699 (alk. paper)
Subjects: LCSH: Early childhood education. |
Teacher-student relationships. |
  Listening. | Communication in education. | Child development.
Classification: LCC LB1139.23 .M348 2019 | DDC 372.21--dc23
LC record available at https://lccn.loc.gov/2018012621

British Library Cataloguing in Publication Data
A CIP catalogue record for this book is available from the British Library

ISBN 978 1 78592 469 9
eISBN 978 1 78450 855 5

Printed and bound in Great Britain

Thank you to Rachel, Claire and Jim
for leading the way in my participation work.
Thank you to Claire, Rachel, Ruth and Fred
for reading, advising and offering thoughts.
Thank you Louie and Victoria for an example
of your wonderful work.

Contents

Introduction

I firmly believe that listening to children is the most important role for the adult working with children. As adults, it is all too easy to presume we know what life is like for a child, but unless we stop, listen and try to see the world through their eyes, we will never know.

Listening to children is so much more than listening to their words; it is about listening and noticing children's behaviours, sounds and facial expressions, their play and their drawings.

Listening to children became my work in 2001. I changed jobs within the large children's charity I was working for and my new job's focus was on children's participation. I was trained as an NNEB and most of my previous work had been with early years, whereas the new job was with 0–18-year-olds. In the interview I was told there would be little if no work with younger children as most participation work was with older children and the commonly held ideology was that younger children were too young to have a view. I remember arguing that we could do some excellent participation work with young children and that they were more than capable of giving their views. Little did I know at the time that the work with participation and younger children was to become an area that I specialised in and one that I would fight hard with the local authority to take seriously. It was to become my world and my passion for many years. Thankfully my manager listened to me and believed me and there were leaders in the council services who agreed with my views. Together we worked on some fantastic projects to hear all children's voices, including the youngest of children in the geographic area.

Legislation

In 2001 the main piece of legislation was the UN Convention on the Rights of the Child (1989) and Article 12 states 'Every child has a right to express their views, feelings, and wishes in all matters affecting them, and to have their views considered and taken seriously. This right applies at all times'.[1] In England, this right was also enshrined in the Children Act 1989. The United Nations Convention on the Rights of the Child (UNCRC) is applicable to all children under the age of 18. The Committee recognised that younger children were often being missed out and for this reason, they implemented a day in 2004 entitled 'Implementing Child Rights in early childhood'.[2] As a follow up to this day the United Nations Committee adopted General Comment 7, which gave an emphasis on the view that young children are also rights holders and that their age does not take this right away. Later in 2013, the UN Committee produced General Comment 14, which again emphasised that young

---

1   www.unicef.org.uk/what-we-do/un-convention-child-rights/
2   https://www.unicef.org/earlychildhood/files/Guide_to_GC7.pdf

children have a right to express their views and be involved in decision making.

Since that time legislation has grown with a greater inclusion and recognition of the need to listen to young children; many local authorities now have polices on how they will do this. There are some great examples across the country of how children of a young age are influencing policy. One of the most positive recent ones I have read about is from Northern Ireland, where young children were consulted over the Early Years (0–6) strategy. However, it also appears that the political tide is turning again, with less of a clear interest and lead from the current government on this. Although many local authorities have these policies, in this time of austerity and cutbacks I fear that we are hearing less about children's voice and children's participation.

Guiding reasons for listening to children

The areas of children's participation and listening to children were my main work for 13 years. Over this time I supported many settings including social services, health, nurseries, schools and children's centres to think about how they embedded a culture of listening to children in their practice. I was fortunate to see some inspiring practice across the UK and to visit and learn from excellent practice in Italy, Denmark, Sweden and Romania. This book draws together my ideas and practice that I have observed and taken part in.

For me there are four important guiding reasons for listening to children:

1. Listening to children acknowledges
   their right to views and ideas now.

2. Listening to children enables us to see
   the world through their eyes.

3. Listening to children helps to give them a
   sense of being special and important.

4. Listening to children helps to enhance their
   wellbeing and helps them to feel they belong.

Participation rights

The view that children have participation rights is a contentious one, with some adults still believing children are too young to have an opinion about things that affect them. An important voice in the world of participation work and children's rights was Hart (1992). He created a diagram called the ladder of participation, (1992, p.8) which looks at different ways children can be involved in decision making and participation. This is a basic model but offers some useful points for reflection about how and why we involve and listen to children. At the bottom of the ladder are three levels of non-participation – manipulation, decoration and tokenism – and at the top of the ladder is child-initiated work. There are some problems with this model as it is very hierarchical, but as an idea it has been very helpful to my work and many others.

In the world of young children's rights and participation, there have been some leading people who have influenced much of the work and development in this area: my own and that of many others too. Penny Lancaster (2003) developed a very influential pack called *Listening to Young Children*; this was full of ideas, theory and practice. Alison Clark and Peter Moss (2001) developed the Mosaic approach, which is about using observations and photographs to enable children to have an involvement in planning. Jacqui Cousins' (1999) work on how teachers and nursery workers can listen to four-year-olds and see the world through their eyes has been very influential.

What is in this book?

This book is about how we listen to children and involve them in decision making in ways that are appropriate to their age and stage of development. It is written in two parts, with the intention that you can either read it as a whole or dip into the chapters you need. The first section looks at what listening to young children is and the types of decisions young children can be involved in. It also looks at policy and legislation and the consequences when we don't listen to children. The second section offers practical ideas and suggestions on how you can listen to children. These are drawn from practice I have been involved in and have observed and the examples include involvement in planning, staff recruitment, transitions, redesigning outdoor spaces and classrooms, community spaces, assessment and family support work. This wide and varied coverage aims to capture the many different ways we can and should be involving and listening to children.

This book is aimed at anyone working with early years children. There are examples which are appropriate for family support workers, social workers, nursery nurses, childminders, teachers and community workers. My hope is that the book will provide you with some ideas on how you can embed listening to children into your daily practice.

References

Clark, A. and Moss, P. (2001) *Listening to Young Children: The Mosaic Approach.* London: National Children's Bureau.

Cousins, J. (1999) *Listening to Four Year Olds: How They Can Help Us Plan Their Education and Care.* London: National Early Years Network.

Hart, R.A. (1992) 'Children's participation: from tokenism to citizenship.' *Innocenti Essays 4.* Florence: UNICEF. Accessed on 20/06/2018 at www.unicef-irc.org/publications/pdf/childrens_participation.pdf

Lancaster, P. (2003) *Listening to Young Children: The Reader.* Buckingham: Open University Press.

Why We Listen to Children

Chapter 1

What is Listening to Children?

So often as adults we presume that we listen to children and that we know how to listen to children. I have been delivering training on listening to young children across the country for the past 15 years and I repeatedly hear people comment, 'Of course we listen; we know how to listen to children, we do it all the time.' However, when we stop and unpick what listening is and reflect on our practice, we realise that listening to children is a skill; it takes time, it's not a quick process and it needs to be an intentional act.

Julia Maria Gouldsboro (2018, p.2) describes the process of listening as: 'adults and children using many different languages and codes to express themselves, this includes moments of pauses, gaps and turn taking'. I love this as it describes beautifully the two-way act of intent and purpose and recognises that it is not just about the words we hear.

Seeing the world through a child's eyes

As adults we cannot presume that we know what a child thinks and feels and what they see. It is only by stopping and listening that we begin to see their world through their eyes.

Questions for practice

Before we continue, take a moment to think about the last time or a recent time you listened to a child, when you really listened and saw the world through their eyes. This might be a child you work with, your own child, a relative or a neighbour's child.

What did you discover in that moment from the child?

How did the experience make the child feel?

How did the experience make you feel?

Every week I work as a nurture consultant with four-year-olds who are finding life and school very challenging. An essential part of my work is to listen to the children I am with, to really hear how it is for them at that moment. Even though this is something I know is vital, I also know that occasionally I do not really listen. Some days I might be feeling busy, or I might be fixed on the work we are doing that day and I miss the opportunity to really listen. It takes an intentional act to stop and really listen to children.

Listening to children isn't just about the physical act of listening; it is also about hearing and acting on their views.

This doesn't mean that we implement everything that children tell us or ask for, but it does require us to consider and count their views alongside those of others (Lancaster 2003).

How much of listening is words?

We know that listening involves more than the words that we hear. So much of listening is also about the non-verbal communication and the tone of voice. How often have you heard a child or an adult say they are fine when they look really sad or their voice is wavering?

It is thought that

- 7 per cent of communication is verbal (the words we say)

- 38 per cent of communication is vocal (tone of voice, inflection)

- 55 per cent of communication is non-verbal (body language, gesture, facial expression).

This formula was devised by Albert Mehrabian (1967).[1] It is a very simple formula and it may not be appropriate for every type of communication situation, but it gives us a broad idea about how we communicate and I think it is quite helpful to think about in the context of listening to children.

1   http://changingminds.org/explanations/behaviors/body_language/mehrabian.htm

Some children we work with cannot express themselves through words. The skill as practitioners is in hearing them in the whole sense, really tuning in to what the child is telling us through their gestures, behaviour, facial expressions and sounds. Audrey Tait and Helen Wosu (2013) describe how children are experts on their own life stories; we just need to listen to what they are telling us and recognise that they do this through words, gestures, drawing and behaviour.

What does listening mean in practice?

There are a few different ways in which we listen to children, these are:

Making an immediate change: responding to need

We do this all the time. When a baby is crying we respond appropriately, for example we change their nappy, feed them or play with them. When a toddler is thirsty we offer them a drink and when a three-year-old wants to play with the trains instead of the dolls, we get these out.

As part of planning

We can do this by involving children in plans for the day; for example a childminder might ask if they want to go to the park or library. We can follow children's interests in our planning, for example by creating a treasure map together and making pirate costumes and boats with a group who are fascinated by pirates. It could also mean including children in the planning of changes to the garden or nursery.

Bigger decision making or involvement in a wider context

This is usually when the children are involved in bigger decisions which may or may not directly involve or affect them. Examples of this are involving children in recruitment and staff appraisals and including children's views in children and young people's plans for the local authority.

Co-production: working on a project which is their idea, their passion

The term co-production is often used in participation work with older children and teenagers; however, there is no reason why this can't be used with younger children. Co-production is when children choose something they want to work on and with support from adults they make it happen. An example of this is children deciding they want to grow some flowers in the garden. They would look at seed catalogues, visit the garden centre, choose the seeds to grow, take them back and plant them. The point of co-production is that children are leading throughout, so as staff you would ask them which garden centre they want to go to, ideas for how they can get there, how they are going to pay for the seeds, and so on.

The practical skills of listening to children

I think it is essential in a book on listening to young children to include a section on observations. As early years practitioners we have a lot of experience of observations; they form an essential part of our work in helping us to understand what the child is enjoying and how they are learning. Observations help us to really understand and get to know the children we are working with. An excellent early years trainer, Kathy Brodie[2] has online training on the subject of observation. She describes observations as really looking and good listening: listening to how the children interact with each other and how they communicate. She suggests observations are about making sense of everything you have gathered; these can then help us to put together a bigger picture of the child, their progress, their interests and their development.

There are a wide variety of observations that we can use. Some of these can include quick sticky note or 'wow moment' observations of what a child likes, comments they have made or an achievement. These can be used for quickly gathering children's ideas; for example, ideas for naming the new pet fish or ideas for lunch. Longer narrative observation can be used when an adult is watching the child for an extended period of time, noticing how they are playing, how they interact with others, any behaviours, what they are playing with and how they are expressing themselves. The longer observations are really useful to capture a deeper understanding of the child. These are not about judgements that you are making but they give you a picture of what you are seeing. In my nurture role, I do around five long observations on a new child: two while they are in nursery and three when they are in school in different situations, for example, in the morning, at lunch time and in the afternoon. These give me a really

---

2   www.kathybrodie.com

good sense of the child; they are a really useful listening tool. I will then do further long observations throughout the term to see the progress the child is making. In Kathy Brodie's observations training (as mentioned above) she recommends using sociogram observations. Kathy describes these as having a focus on the social interactions and the physical environment. They are represented on a diagram because social interactions can be complex and sometimes fleeting and happen in many physical places. This style of observation is such a useful tool, really aiding practitioners to gain a fuller understanding of how a child is in a setting, for example where they play, whether they flit and who they play and interact with. I have found this to be one of the most useful observation tools for understanding and tracking a child's social development. Fawcett (2009) also explores the many different types of observations and explains how to use them in her book.

In Chapter 3, I mention the importance of noticing and observing when a child's behaviour is changing, and how this can sometimes be an indication to us that the child is unhappy or something is wrong. We are able to use observations of our very youngest children in evidence when we are submitting information for assessments, for example for an early help assessment. In most parts of the country, early help assessments have replaced the common assessment framework (CAF); they are similar but a slightly adapted form and some argue they are easier to use with families. This has come about since the recommendation in the Eileen Munro review (Cooper 2011). I know of one nursery that submitted a video observation of a two-year-old as part of the old CAF assessment; this provided the team with really useful evidence and they were able to see and hear the child directly for themselves.

A definition of listening to children

When I deliver training on listening to children, I often ask groups to devise their own definition of listening. This is a useful exercise as it gives time to reflect on what we mean by listening. I have recently been delivering training on the Wirral to children centre workers; a couple of definitions they wrote were:

> Listening is active participation in absorbing a message through hearing, seeing and feeling expressive communication.
>
> Listening is an active process where we see, hear, feel and respond to what is being communicated.

Coming up with a definition for listening is a useful team exercise to do: thinking of a definition for your team, of what you mean by listening. When we stop and reflect on it, we realise listening really is layered.

Stages in the development of children communicating with us

As we know babies are born with an ability to communicate. From the moment they are born they are able to tell us through their many varied sounds – snuffling, whimpers, their cries – that they need changing, feeding, comforting, cuddling, walking, or to have calming shushing noises made to them. They are able to follow us with their eyes and respond to familiar voices. Our role as adults is to interpret what the baby is telling us and to meet their needs and to love them. In *The Social Baby* (Murray and Andrews 2005) they show a photo sequence of a baby who has just been born and is being held and gazed at by his dad. The dad pokes his tongue out and the baby watches intently; the dad repeats this and the baby copies. This is a beautiful piece of footage of showing us how babies are communicating from birth.

Below are some examples of ways that young children are able to communicate to us and choices that they make. There is of course a broad range of development and it will vary for each individual child.

Babies from birth to three months have different cries for different varying needs, for example their tired cry is different from their hungry cry. The key is for the adult to tune in and understand what the cry is telling us. Babies quickly learn to coo and make noises of pleasure. Within a few weeks, they begin to smile. From birth babies love faces and watching intently; as described above, they will stick out their tongues to copy what they are seeing. Babies often have whole-body reactions to communicate with the people around them, waving their arms and legs.

Babies from around four to six months begin to make more noises, giggle and squawk; they begin to make early sounds and babbling. They increase their ability to reach and grasp for toys, hair and things they want to explore. They start to show early preference for things and people.

Babies around six to nine months increase their ability and intent to choose the toy they want to reach and move towards or which person they want to be with, for example, reaching out for Mum or Dad, sister or grandparent. They are able to point, make noises and smile to get attention and communicate. They begin to communicate using gestures such as waving and flapping their arms. Babies of around six months listen to speech sounds, they start to turn towards people talking and are able recognise their name and pay attention when they hear their name.

Babies around nine months are able to show preference in the food you give them, for example giggling and laughing while eating some banana and screwing up their faces and spitting out avocado. Babies at this age are sitting up and reaching out for objects and toys; they are beginning to be able to pick up small objects and are showing their curiosity and interest in everything around them. From around nine months they can choose where they move to, rolling, crawling or walking (dependent on their development) across rooms and towards people or objects. They continue to show us what they enjoy and what they want through a growing range of sounds, for example grunts, squeals, early sounds of words, growls, giggles and chuckles.

These are all examples of early ways babies are communicating with us, telling us their preferences and their needs, showing us what they want.

From one to two years toddlers are learning how to move, becoming proficient in walking and running. They are making clear choices about what they want and don't want, the toy (or item) they want to play with, the place they want to explore and the food they want to eat. They are learning words; often an early word they learn is 'no'.

From two years onwards children are able to communicate their strong preferences; they can choose the clothes they want to wear, whether they want to play inside or outside and whether they want the red plate or the blue plate. They can show and tell you through vocalisations and gesture that they want a certain toy or don't want someone else to have it. They can begin to show you and tell you from two years what toys they like.

This ability to show us their preferences and their choices develops as they continue to grow and develop. This section isn't intended as a full description of child development, but to give some insight into how children are communicating with us from birth and how they develop making choices and early decisions. We can see that the sometimes held view that children are unable to make choices is a false one.

To learn more about the developmental stages of young children Kathy Brodie's (2018) book on holistic care and development of children from birth to three is a useful read.

Questions for practice

Think about the children you work with. What choices are you helping them to make? Some ideas to think about:

- Do they have a choice at snack time, for example, two things to choose from?
- How do you enable them to choose what they play with?
- Do you use song baskets at singing time, with toys or pictures representing the songs and enabling children to choose the songs?

- ◼ Do you have free flow inside and outside or; if not, are there opportunities for children to choose to be inside or outside?
- ◼ Can they choose if, when and where they can sleep?
- ◼ Do they help buy new resources for the setting?
- ◼ Do you follow their interests and ideas as part of your planning?

Active listening

Listening to children is an intentional act; it requires an active response. To listen to children there are a few basic ways we need to behave:

- We need to stop what we are doing.

- Ideally we should get to a child's height and if possible get eye contact.

- Look at the child, watch their body language and facial expression as well the words they are using.

- Don't interrupt.

- Check back with the child what you have heard; sometimes we have not understood what they are trying to tell us.

- Where possible, act on what the child has told you.

Reflection model

When we are working on a project with children around listening to their ideas, it is useful to use a reflective model in our practice. There is a useful model of refection from Kolb (1984)[3] which is widely used. The Kolb model involves:

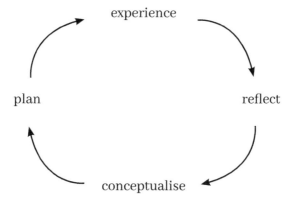

- A way of using the model in listening to children's projects is by asking the following questions:What do we want to know from the children?

- How are we going to find out?

- How will we document what they have told us and what we have learnt?

- How will we action the children's ideas?

- How will we feed back to the children?

Sometimes it can be useful to use this model in team meetings or supervision as a way of planning, thinking and reflecting on the work you are doing.

---

3   http://skillsforlearning.leedsbeckett.ac.uk/preview/content/ models/02.shtml

References

Brodie, K. (2018) *The Holistic Care and Development of Children from Birth to Three*. Abingdon: Routledge.

Cooper, J. (2011) Munro: Early intervention legal duty for councils. Accessed on 14/06/2018 at: www.communitycare.co.uk/2011/05/10/munro-early-intervention-legal-duty-for-councils.

Fawcett, M. (2009) *Learning through Child Observation*. London: Jessica Kingsley Publishers.

Gouldsboro, J.M. (2018) *The Voice of the Child:, How to Listen Effectively to Young Children*. Oxford: David Fulton.

Lancaster, P. (2003) *Listening to Young Children: The Reader*. Buckingham: Open University Press.

Murray, L. and Andrews, L. (2005) *The Social Baby: Understanding Babies Communication from Birth*. London: CP Publishing.

Tait, A. and Wosu, H. (2013) *Direct Work with Vulnerable Children: Playful Activities and Strategies for Communication*. London: Jessica Kingsley Publishers.

Chapter 2

The Policy of Listening to Young Children

In a book on listening to young children, it is important to look at the policy and legislation around this subject, which has grown over the years.

The policy and legislation around this subject have increased since 2001 when I began working in this area. Putting children's voices into policy ensures the rights of all children to be listened to in law. These are laws which we are all working to. This chapter is going to look briefly at the policy and legislation currently in place in the UK.

United Nations Convention on the Rights of the Child (UNCRC)

For me this is the most important piece of legislation we have. It is easy to take it for granted, but I believe it is a very influential piece of legislation that has led the way to the other legislation we have in the UK. The United Nations general assembly adopted the UNCRC in November 1989 and it came into force on 2 September 1990. The convention came into force in the UK in 1992. This is a legally binding international agreement, which sets out the civil, political, economic, social and cultural rights of every child. The UNCRC has 54 articles that identify children's rights and how governments need to work together to make sure they are available to all children.[1]

Since the adoption of the UNCRC in 1989, all UN member states have ratified it apart from the United States of America. A list of all countries that have ratified it and when this happened can be found on the Unicef website.[2]

The Convention requires governments to meet children's basic needs and enable them to reach their full potential. It recognises all children's basic fundamental rights. All children have the right to:

- life, including growing and developing
- protection from abuse, neglect and violence
- an education that enables all children to meet their potential
- live with or have a relationship with their family
- express their views and opinions and be listened to.

Guiding principles

The articles in the UNCRC fall under three categories or guiding principles.The right to:

---

1   www.savethechildren.org.uk/about-us/what-we-do/child-rights/un-convention-on-the-rights-of-the-child
2   https://treaties.un.org/pages/viewdetails.aspx?src=treaty&mtdsg_no=iv-11&chapter=4&lang=en

- provision

- protection

- participation.

Article 12

The article in the UNCRC that underpins all work around listening to children is article 12. This states: 'Every child has a right to express their views, feelings, and wishes in all matters affecting them, and to have their views considered and taken seriously. This right applies at all times.'[3]

Article 12 affirms that children are people with their own rights now, that they have the right to express their thoughts and views in everything that affects them and that these views need to be heard, considered and given due weight in accordance with the child's age and maturity.[4] This does not mean that children's views need to be automatically put into place, but it does mean they need to be carefully listened to, considered and taken into account. In my role as a participation worker, we had a phrase we used: 'It is not about children always having their way but it is about children always having their say.' When we ask children for their views, we then need to ensure that we always feed back to them. I will refer to this more throughout the book.

3   www.unicef.org.uk/what-we-do/un-convention-child-rights/
4   www.unicef.org/crc/files/Right-to-Participation.pdf

Feedback

One of the important aspects of this legislation is the way it holds countries to account. It is not just a case of a country signing it and then ignoring it. When a country signs up to the UNCRC this means the government will ensure that all areas of the government and the state will do everything they can to ensure children's rights are met and fulfilled. This includes education, local government, health services and criminal justice. Every five years the country needs to tell the UN how they are implementing these rights. The UN then examine and feed back on improvements that could be made. Each country is held to account by the UN.

In June 2016 the UK government was examined by the UN committee on how well they were meeting and complying with the UNCRC. The UN gave feedback and passed on concerns and recommendations on how the UK government can change. A list of these can be found on the Children's Rights Alliance for England website (CRAE)[5] and the official feedback letter can be found online.[6] The recommendations from the UN included:

- a call for the UK government to implement a child rights action plan

- a call for the Government to develop, fund and implement a plan to reduce the number of children in poverty year on year over the next five years

---

5   www.crae.org.uk/media/120204/CRAE_SCR2016_B1_EXEC-SUMMARY_WEB.pdf

6   www.equalityhumanrights.com/sites/default/files/letter-to-edward-timpson-concluding-observations-un-committee-rights-child-september-2016.pdf

- a call for the Government to ring fence 1.4 billion investment into Child and Adolescent Mental Health Services (CAMHS).

As adults working with children we have a responsibility to ensure we embed children's rights into our daily practice; we also have a responsibility to inform children about their rights. There are many good websites and resources for children. For younger children the book *For Every Child* (Various 2002) is a beautifully illustrated picture book explaining children's rights.

The Education Act

In 2002 The Education Act under section 176[7] states that all pupils are to be involved in consultation in connection with decisions that affect them; this is within the context of the child's age and understanding. In 2014 guidance was developed from the Department of Education[8] on how this could be implemented. The guidance explains in a simple way why children should be listened to. It suggests that listening to children enables them to become active participants within their school and democratic society and that it can contribute to achievement and attainment. Interestingly the Education Act states that 'pupils' do not include a child being provided with nursery education.

Although this is in our legislation I am not convinced it is always being kept to. I don't know if many, or even any,

7   www.legislation.gov.uk/ukpga/2002/32/section/176
8   www.gov.uk/government/uploads/system/uploads/attachment_data/file/437241/Listening_to_and_involving_children_and_young_people.pdf

children were consulted over the new Free schools, Multi Academy Trusts and so on that we are seeing throughout England.

The Children Act 2004 and Childcare Act 2006

The Children Act 2004[9] was a piece of legislation which saw the introduction of the Children's Commissioner for England. The Children's Commissioner's initial role was to promote the views and interests of children and young people, to find out what they think and to encourage decision makers to take children's and young people's views into account. Since 2014 the Commissioner also has special responsibility for the rights of children in the care system.[10]

There was also the Childcare Act in 2006; this was the first legislation exclusively concerned with early years and childcare. In section 3.5[11] it states that the voices of young children need to be listened to and actively taken into account. It also states they need to be seen as partners in planning and commissioning of services. It states that when local authorities take on consultation around early childhood services they have to consider and act on how they include the voices of young children.

The Childcare Act 2006 was an important piece of legislation when it first came into place. In 2006 I worked

---

9   www.legislation.gov.uk/ukpga/2004/31/pdfs/ukpga_20040031_en.pdf

10 https://www.childrenscommissioner.gov.uk/about-us/the-childrens-commissioner-for-england/

11 www.legislation.gov.uk/ukpga/2006/21/pdfs/ukpga_20060021_en.pdf

as a participation worker for a large children's charity. As a team we were commissioned by our local authority to run participation work. As part of this I was involved in working with the early years team to involve young children in the commissioning and setting up of new children centres. At that time there were some great examples across the country of different authorities putting this into practice, seeing and involving children as planners alongside the adults. Sadly, I fear this has begun to slip away, particularly in this time of austerity and budget cuts.

Early Years Foundation Stage (EYFS)

The EYFS places a strong emphasis on listening to children, children's participation and the involvement of young children in decision making. The EYFS practice guidance from 2008 states that 'all children are listened to and respected'.[12] The Development Matters document gives examples of children making decisions and having choices. In 8–20 months under personal, social, emotional development: within self-confidence and self-awareness; it recommends that where possible staff give opportunities for babies to have choices.[13]

---

12   http://webarchive.nationalarchives.gov.uk/20130321061316/https://
www.education.gov.uk/publications/eOrderingDownload/DCSF-
00266-2008.pdf

13   www.foundationyears.org.uk/files/2012/03/Development-Matters-
FINAL-PRINT-AMENDED.pdf

Questions for practice

How do you talk to children about their rights?

Do you have a copy of the book *For Every Child*? (See the References below.)

When you are making large changes, such as adding a new building or developing outdoor areas, how do you involve children? According to the Education and Childcare Act we all have a responsibility to do this.

Reference

Various (2002) *For Every Child.* Wiltshire: Red Fox.

Chapter 3

The Consequences of Not Listening to Children

I believe it is important to consider the consequences of not listening to children. This chapter does come with a warning as some of the things we look at here are distressing. However, it is important that we recognise what can happen when we don't listen to children.

Serious case reviews

We know through reading many serious case reviews that the consequences of not listening to children are huge and can lead to death or serious injury. It is due to this realisation and on the back of the Waterhouse report – a North Wales Child Abuse Tribunal[1] based on child abuse in the 1970s and 1980s in care homes – that Penny Lancaster (2003) was commissioned to create the *Listening to Young*

---

1   http://online.carmarthenshire.gov.uk/agendas/eng/SCSC20000929/
     REP15.htm

Children training pack. At the time of the Waterhouse report it was suggested that if the children had been listened to then the abuse they experienced by their carers could have been limited and possibly prevented (Lancaster 2003). Sadly, since then there have continued to be many serious case reviews where it has been identified that children were not listened to, were not asked what was happening and did not have their views taken seriously. The following two examples are of cases where adults failed children and young people by not listening to them.

Victoria Climbié

This is the tragic case of an eight-year-old girl, Victoria Climbié, who was neglected, physically harmed and killed by her aunt and her aunt's partner in 2000. There was later an inquiry led by Lord Laming[2] which led to significant changes within care and education and led to the intro-duction of Every Child Matters[3] and an expectation on all agencies to communicate and share information. Every Child Matters was a vital new piece of legislation at the time as it brought all children services under one grouping within local authorities. This forced all agencies who worked with children to communicate and work together, which sounds obvious but was so often missing in practice. The issue of interprofessional working was also later highlighted in the Munro review of child protection in 2011.

---

2   www.gov.uk/government/uploads/system/uploads/attachment_data/
     file/273183/5730.pdf

3   www.gov.uk/government/uploads/system/uploads/attachment_data/
     file/272064/5860.pdf

A key element in Victoria's case was that she was seen by many different agencies and professionals. Victoria was not a hidden child; from April 1999 when she arrived in the UK to her death in February 2000 she was known to two housing agencies, four social services teams, two police child protection teams and a centre run by the NSPCC, and was admitted to two hospitals due to suspected deliberate harm. It is believed that there were 12 key occasions when services could have intervened. One key issue was the lack of communication between agencies (Laming 2003). Another was that no one asked Victoria about her injuries and no one enquired about how she was, how she felt or if she had any worries or concerns. The main reason given in response to this was that she spoke French and the agencies did not have an interpreter. When they did ask her anything they used the aunt to interpret.

Victoria's is such a tragic case and it is easy to use the excuse of her speaking French as an explanation for why she was not listened to. However, we sadly know that even with the increased training around child protection and greater communication between agencies, there are still many examples of children dying and the adults working with them not listening or questioning .

Thematic Oftsed report looking at the voice of the child in serious case reviews

A thematic Ofsted report was released in 2011 which looked at the voice of the child and lessons learnt from serious case reviews (Ofsted 2011). This was on the back of the Munro (2011) report into child protection services. This Ofsted report looked at 67 serious case reviews between 1 April and 30 September 2010. One of the key findings was that professionals did not see children enough and children were not asked their views and feelings. In a summary[4] of five serious case reviews published in September that year, including Daniel Pelka[5] (aged four years) and Keanu Williams[6] (two years), the review found that one common theme was that the child's voice and their experience were not central to the practice or central to the consideration of each of the cases.

Unfortunately this still isn't improving. In 2016 a serious case review into the death of Christopher Ostle, a three-month-old baby, found that due to the complex mental health needs of the mother, Christopher's voice and those of his sibling were not listened to. Professionals were found guilty of 'lacking curiosity'; they didn't try to find out what the lived daily experience was for the children (Stevenson 2016).

We are all responsible for listening to children and safeguarding

Each of us working with children and young people has a responsibility for safeguarding; we all know this as we are all trained in this area. Sometimes it can be easy to miss the child's voice in our work.

4   www.trixonline.co.uk/website/news/pdf/policy_briefing_No-99.pdf

5   www.lgiu.org.uk/wp-content/uploads/2013/10/Daniel-Pelka-Serious-Case-Review-Coventry-LSCB.pdf

6   www.gov.uk/government/uploads/system/uploads/attachment_data/file/272064/5860.pdf

One of my jobs is as a nurture consultant. I work for a team in Bath called Threeways, Brighter Futures and I am part of their Nurture Outreach Service, a service that supports Reception-aged children in their transition from pre-school to school throughout their Reception year and across the transition into Year 1. Some of the children I support are on child protection plans and some are children in need.

An essential element in my role with all the children I work with, whether they are known to social services or not, is to really listen to what they are telling us. Sometimes this is clear with a child disclosing but at other times it is not; it is about observing and noticing, for example, if a child's behaviour changes, if they start to look different in some way or if their language changes. It is not always the big or obvious things that are significant. In these situations I discuss with other staff what I am seeing and I speak with the child. It's not unusual for the child to not disclose or not discuss what they are feeling. I also make a note in my records of changes I have noticed; this can act as a useful tool to go back to and track the changes. Schools keep records of ongoing concerns and obviously where social services or other agencies are involved we share concerns.

The key is to listen with all our senses to what the child is telling us; we know it is not just about the words children say but also how they behave and how they look. When a child's behaviour or their appearance changes this is for a reason; this is telling us something and we need to listen and act.

As mentioned in Chapter 2, listening to children is not just about hearing the voices of older children; it is about listening to all children, whatever their age and ability. In our regular supervision practice we should have an allocated slot about what are we hearing from children. In my last team we also had this as an agenda item on our monthly team meeting agendas. On our assessment forms, we should have a section which asks for the views of the child and we should never leave this blank or comment that the child was too young.

This chapter has given examples of what can happen if we don't listen and act on what we are hearing from children. This is a sobering and frightening thought, but the flip side to this is that by listening to children, we can change their lives for the better. Tait and Wosu (2013) describe how in every interaction with a child we have the ability to change their world view of adults; the healing process for children can begin by adults believing in them, listening to them, engaging with them. This brings so much hope; we can be that hope for the children we work with.

Questions for practice

How do you ensure you are hearing and acting on the voice of child in your work?

When a child's behaviour changes are you asking the questions: What is happening for the child right now? What are they trying to tell me?

References

Laming, W. (2003) The Victoria Climbie inquiry. Accessed on 18/06/2018 at http://lx.iriss.org.uk/sites/default/files/resources/113A.%20The%20 Victoria%20Climbie%20Inquiry%20-%20Summary-Report.pdf

Lancaster, P. (2003) *Listening to Young Children: The Reader.* Buckingham: Open University Press.

Ofsted (2011) The voice of the child: learning lessons from serious case reviews. Accessed on 18/06/2018 at www.bucks-lscb.org.uk/wp-content/uploads/Serious_Case_Reviews/Ofsted_Report_The_Voice_of_the_Child.pdf

Munro, E. (2011) The Munro review of child protection final report. Accessed on 15/12/17 at https://assets.publishing.service.gov.uk/government/uploads/system/uploads/attachment_data/file/175391/Munro-Review.pdf

Tait,A. and Wosu, H. (2013) *Direct Work with Vulnerable Children: Playful Activities and Strategies for Communication.* London: Jessica Kingsley Publishers.

Stevenson, L. (2016) Voice of children not heard in case where baby died, review says. Accessed on 18/06/2018 at http://www.communitycare.co.uk/2016/11/22/voice-children-heard-case-child-died-review-says/

How We Listen to Children

Chapter 4

Children's Voice in Recruitment

In many schools, it is now normal good practice to involve children in the recruitment of new staff. Within the voluntary sector, this has been viewed as good practice for a long time. Originally this was a much more common practice with senior schools and in work with young people; however, this is becoming increasingly popular in early years. I am always disappointed when I hear of organisations that don't involve children and young people in staff recruitment. I firmly believe that if a job involves working with children and young people, then they should be included in the recruitment process.

We know that taking care in our staff recruitment is important with regards to safeguarding; by involving children in staff recruitment you are giving a clear message that you take listening to children very seriously, which is a safeguarding expectation.

I have been fortunate to be involved in supporting children and young people in staff recruitment for many years. I have worked with children from aged two to

18 years in staff recruitment for many different jobs and I have had the privilege to be interviewed by children and young people.

By involving children in staff recruitment you are acknowledging that they have a right to a say in who works with them. You are acknowledging that they are able to give their views and opinions and that these have a place for consideration alongside those of the adult panel.

From my experience I have found children and young people to be very insightful when it comes to recruitment; they will often ask the questions that the adults are unsure of asking, they are often able to see candidates for who they really are and they regularly put candidates at their ease, far more than adults do. If we are expecting people to be able to work with children and young people then they should not be fazed by being interviewed by them. Sometimes children will ask left field questions; my favourite is 'If you were an animal, what animal would you be?'; however, if you are confident in working with children then you should be able to confidently and honestly answer their questions of any kind.

When involving children in any type of staff recruitment you need to be very sensitive to the needs of the children. You need to get their consent on this; if they clearly do not want to take part in an activity this must always be respected. However, I think involving children in staff recruitment has massive benefits.

There are many different ways to involve children in staff recruitment; the suggestions that follow are ones I have used over the years.

Person specification (children aged two and over)

Involving children in the person specification is a great a way to begin including children's views in staff recruitment. On the person specification, there can be a section which states 'Children in our setting would like a person to...'. For this section you could do some work with the children around the qualities they would like to see in a new worker:

- You could do this as a small group discussion around what makes a good key person/room leader/teacher.

- You could draw around an adult in the room on large paper and write the children's ideas of what they want a new person to be like on the outline. Children have come up with things such as kind, good at fixing toys, good at reading stories, can play football, can climb a tree. It will be different for every group of children.

You would then include these comments, in the children's words, on the person specification. These are activities that would need to be used for each new worker and the ideas from the children may change over time.

Example of children's ideas for a person specification
The children in our nursery told us they want a worker who can:
- read stories and use funny voices
- make gloop

- tell jokes
- climb a tree.

Interview panel (children aged three and over)

Many schools use this format, having a children's panel alongside the adults' as part of the recruitment process. I have used this in primary schools to recruit head teachers, teachers, teaching assistants and lunchtime staff; I have also used it in the voluntary sector.

When using an interview panel it is very important to prepare children properly for this. This preparation takes time so do not rush it; I usually do this over a few days. Part of the preparation is to explain simply to children how interviews work: what happens, how we ask questions, why we interview and how we score candidates. First, have a conversation about what type of person the children want and how they will know if the candidate is like that. It is also important to talk about making decisions on what the candidates have told us not on what they are wearing or how they look. This last one is important; I once had two children score highly based on the 'pretty pink cardigan' that the candidate wore! In this instance I had forgotten to explain to the children why we don't do that. However, children are often very good at noticing and picking up on strengths and weakness of staff and will often ask some excellent questions.

You also need to explain to the children how their views will form part of the final decision. They need to be told that their chosen person may not be the person who gets the job but their views *will* be carefully considered.

When recruiting with children you do learn things from experience. Following one particular instance I have learnt to check that the children have understood what I said. I was preparing children in a small primary school for interviewing a head teacher and told them we would score the candidates. I discovered they all thought we scored in the way they did on Strictly Come Dancing; they were all very disappointed that they were not going to be holding up a three, a seven or a ten! I guess this could be one way of interviewing although I think as a candidate seeing that you scored a three or a one could be very off-putting!

Guidelines for the recruitment process

- Explain to the children how interviews work, what their role is going to be and how their votes will count.
- The children then come up with a list of questions that they will ask.
- Together agree which children will ask the questions (one question for each child is ideal).
- In a primary or infant school, it can work well to have an older child supporting a younger child, for example a Year 2 child with a Reception child.
- Agree how you are going to score and have a simple score sheet on clipboards for children to use. I often use a range of one to three or one to five.
- After each candidate, have a conversation with the children about what they thought. Write these comments down as they are useful combined with the scoring.

■ Feed back to the children at the end of the process about the final decision.

■ Reward the children involved in the interview panel in some way to say thank you. This could be a certificate or a special afternoon tea.

Questions from children for adult panel (children aged two and over)

I know some nurseries and children centres that ask children for questions to use at the interview. They don"t actually get the children to ask the questions but they are used by the panel. The staff ask the children what type of answer they think the candidate should give. This is a very simple way of involving children's ideas and it helps us as adults to find out from children what is important to them in a worker. I have heard questions such as: what is your favourite book? Do you know how to make a paper aeroplane? Will you let me climb trees? Staff need to give feedback to children on how their questions were answered by the person who got the job.

Activity for children (children aged 18 months and over)

Many early years settings choose to do this as part of the recruitment process, setting the task for each candidate of planning and carrying out an activity with a small group of children. This enables you as managers to observe how the candidates are with children and how the children respond to them. You can also see the type of activity they choose and how appropriate it is for the age/stage of the children.

When you do this it is important to have one person from the panel of recruiters observing the activity. At the end, they then need to have a conversation with the children involved about their thoughts on the activity. I would ask:

- Did you like the activity?

- Did anything about the activity make you happy?

- Did anything about the activity make you sad?

- What did you think of the person?

Use the comments from the children as well as your observation to feed into the panel and decision-making process and ensure you provide feedback to the children about their involvement.

Observation with children (children from birth)

In baby and toddler rooms or groups, many early years settings ask candidates to spend time (around half an hour) in the room. This is an opportunity to see how the candidate responds to the children and how the children respond to the candidate. When you do this it is important to have one person from the panel of recruiters observing this and feeding back to the panel.

I would be looking for the following in the candidate's behaviour:

- How sensitive is the candidate to the children, for example, do they allow children to come to them or do they invade children's space?

- Do they introduce themselves to the children?

- Do they play?

- Do they make eye contact with the children?

From the children I would be looking at the following:

- How do they appear around the person; are they happy and at ease?

- Do any seem unsure or distressed and how does the candidate respond to this?

Of course, it is tricky introducing a new person into the room and some children may be very unhappy about this; as practitioners you need to know the children in your room and how they are with new people. You also need to be very sensitive about how many candidates you bring into a room on one day; I wouldn't have more than two in a day and I would have a big time gap between them, respecting that this is the babies' or children's space.

Staff appraisal (children aged two and over)

Early years settings should be using both supervision and yearly staff appraisals. Over the last five years of my job with the children's charity we used children's comments in our staff appraisals. One of my roles in that job was to manage our gypsy and traveller play work; we had a tiny play bus that we took onto gypsy and traveller sites to run play sessions. In our early years groups I asked our children to tell me about their play workers.

I told the children what the workers needed to do in their job, for example:

- play with children

- keep children on the bus safe

- give the children food and drink.

I asked the children :

- What did...do well in her job?

- What could...get better at in her job?

- Did...keep the children on the bus safe?

- Did they have anything else to tell me?

I loved asking for children's comments in staff appraisal. I also did this when I was chair of governors for the head teachers I worked with. Children are wonderful at finding positives and giving positive comments but they are also really insightful. One group of children with learning disabilities I worked with told my manager I needed to get better at directions because when I drove them on trips I often got lost and they were totally right!

By involving children in staff appraisals as a manager you get to hear directly from children about their experience of the worker; as a worker and a manager this can be very useful and often very affirming. Even when a member of staff is struggling, children will often find something kind and encouraging to say.

Questions for practice

Think about how you do staff recruitment in your setting. Do you involve children in this practice? If not, why not?

Are there things in the list of suggestions that you haven't tried and would like to?

In your staff recruitment policy do you state your commitment to involving children in staff recruitment?

Chapter 5

Children's Voice in Transition

We know that preparing children for transitions is immensely important. There is some excellent writing on transitions to school and how to prepare children for them. In 2017 Anne O'Connor updated her book about understanding transitions in the early years and supporting attachment and resilience; this is an excellent book which addresses many of the difficulties and issues around transitions. In my role as a nurture consultant I spend a lot of time talking and thinking about transitions. The children we work with have been identified as needing high level transition support as they enter school, throughout the year and into Year 1. Tamsin Grimmer (2018) has written an excellent and comprehensive book on school readiness and how we can help children in this important transition.

Over the years I have learnt that as adults we often presume we know what children need to know or what is important to them; however when we stop and listen, and see the world through their eyes, then the view can be different to our own. As adults we may think we know what children need in their transition support, but if we stop and ask them we may hear different priorities. One little girl I worked with who was transitioning to school was very calm and happy about the teacher, the children and the playtime but she was really scared about the lunchtime; there were some foods she really hated and she thought she would be made to eat everything in school dinners. Through hearing her concerns and conversations with school and the parents, it was agreed she wouldn't have school lunches. This took away a very big stress for her and helped her to feel calmer. This chapter is going to offer ways in which we can involve children in transitions and hear from them their worries, concerns and excitement.

The many transitions a child experiences

Within early years we are now giving much more attention to the transition into nursery and into school, recognising how this change can cause many children to feel vulnerable, scared and anxious. However we don't always give as much attention to other transitions, such as moving from the baby room to the toddler room or pre-school room in nursery, or the many transitions a child has in the day, including leaving their parent, moving to the lunch room and going outside. Kathy Brodie (2018) describes these smaller transitions as micro-transitions, and recognises that these can also be very emotional for children.

The other transition that I am particularly concerned about is the one from Reception to Year 1. This is perhaps the biggest transition a child faces as the current Year 1 curriculum is so different to the EYFS. In many Year 1 classes there is much less play than in the EYFS. Unfortunately, in my experience, not enough preparation is given to children for the transition to Year 1. There is a fantastic book looking at how you can carefully manage the transition into Year 1 by Alistair Bryce-Clegg (2017). Also Anne Ephgrave (2017) shows how it is possible to take early years pedagogy into Year 1. They both argue that when this is followed it makes a massive difference to the transition experience of those children. Unfortunately in our current political climate this does not seem to be recognised enough and there are worrying discussions around making Reception more like Year 1, with less play. I feel this would be a detrimental step and would have a serious effect on the wellbeing of Reception children.

When we involve children in transitions – when we talk to them, listen to them, prepare them – we are helping their wellbeing immensely.

Using consultation story books (children aged three and over)

One format I have used for different types of consultation with children is a consultation story book. I first used this method on a project for my undergraduate dissertation linked with a transition project I was doing with the local authority I was based in. The aim of this project was to work with a small group of children and find out what they thought about school, what their worries and concerns were and how much they knew about school. For this project I wrote a resource in a simple story format about a girl called Lily who was starting school. The story told the children about what Lily would wear, which school she was going to, what she would do at lunch times, who her teacher would be and which friends were in her class. It also talked about what she was excited about and what scared her. Each page had a statement about Lily going to school with an appropriate picture and a question for the child

Example of questions from the school story

Lily is going to her new school, it is called Camerton Primary. Where are you going to school?

Lily's school jumper is blue. What colour will your school jumper be?

Lily is going to school with her friend Megan. Which friends are going to your new school?

Lily will be going to school on the bike with her Dad. How will you get to school?

Lily will be having school lunches at school. She likes eating jacket potato. What will you do at lunch time?

Lily is looking forward to playing with the pirate boat in the classroom. What are you looking forward to at school?

Lily is a little bit worried about playtimes, the playground has a big climbing frame and she is a bit scared about that. Does anything worry you about school?

When I first used this format, it very quickly showed us how much the children knew and it gave us a chance to hear the children's worries, concerns and what they were excited about. It was a very simple exercise but one which enabled us to have a conversation and hear from the children their concerns and worries. One of the children in the first group of children I worked with had Down syndrome and communicated through Makaton. I was able to ask him the questions using Makaton and show him the pictures in the book and he was able to join in with the conversations. Through doing the work we realised that one child in the group wasn't very well prepared for the move to school; her mum had not yet bought her uniform or talked to her about school lunches. This highlighted to us the extra support the family needed. Using this format with another child I was able to hear that they were very worried about toilets (this often causes concerns) and we were able to do some extra support with them, including taking photos of the toilets, going into the toilets and hearing the noise they made.

Since making this resource it has been used with many children in nurseries and families have used it at home. This is a very simple idea which can be adapted and easily made by anyone. You could also make something similar about starting nursery.

Children making booklets/information for the new children coming into the group/ class/room (children aged two and over)

One project I have carried out with groups of children over the years is to get children to make a booklet for the new children coming into their class, room or nursery. Often as adults we think we are aware of what children and parents need to know, but when you speak with children they have many other additional ideas. When I worked on this with a Reception class, the first thing the children said we needed to include was a picture and words about the toilets. The words they wanted to use were: 'You ask to go to the toilet. Don't be scared of the flush. It is outside of the classroom. You wash your hands in the sink.'

This is a lovely project to work on. It can be started at any time of the year; it could be used to welcome new children coming into the classroom or nursery throughout the year and can be used for the cohort coming in during the September transition time. This doesn't need to be expensive or fancy; a photocopiable or printable booklet made of a few pages produced on a computer is fine. Some groups include photos taken by the children; others use a mix of photos and children's drawings. Some groups give a copy of the booklet to all new children coming in, encouraging them to take it home and look at it with their family in the lead up to starting school/nursery. Other groups use it as tool to show children when they arrive for a look around. There are cost implications to the first option, but where settings do this the children are often thrilled to receive it and parents often talk about how they looked at it frequently with their child before the transition and how much it helped the child to be prepared.

A project like this could be used for children going into a nursery room, a childminder could make one with their children for new arrivals, a Reception class could make one for the new children arriving at school and a Year 1 class could make it for the Reception children moving into Year 1.

Suggestions for making a booklet with children

The aim of the booklet is to give each child arriving something that they can take home to help them in transition.

- Start by explaining to the children as a group that you are all going to make a booklet for new children coming into the school/nursery/room.
- Talk about how they felt when they first arrived at school/nursery.
- Find out from the children what they think the new children need to know.
- Ask the children what photos or pictures they would like to take/draw of the room/setting to be included in the booklet.
- Use the children's words in the booklet.

Photo/video projects (children aged two and over)

One of the activities we carry out each year as part of the Nurture Outreach Service is a photo/video project with the children we work with. Early in the spring term we get the children to take photos or a video (or both) of what makes them happy in school. We explain to the children that we will use this to tell their new Year 1 teachers about what they like and to help the new teachers to know a little about them. The children love doing this activity; they have lots of fun going around the school and classroom taking photos of the things they enjoy. When they have done this we then look together at the photos/videos the children have taken and we talk about the images and why they took them. As a worker I then collate the photos and the child's comments into a simple booklet, or if we have a video I download it onto a secure sharing space; sometimes I do both photos and video. Together with the child I then show this booklet or video to their current teaching assistant and teacher. This is a lovely way for the staff to be able to listen to the child and really see the classroom/school through their eyes. We also show this to the new Year 1 teacher later in the year, once it is known who their teacher will be.

The benefit of doing a photo/video project is that it enables you to really view the environment through the child's eyes. One child we worked with made a film. The first thing we all saw as the child walked into school was the blank wall of the Reception desk. This has also happened with children's centres where children film the entry to the centre and all they see are blank walls. We are often excellent at putting displays above children's eye height; seeing the environment through the child's eyes can help us re-think our spaces.

Doing a project like this is particularly beneficial for children who you know are going to find the transition especially hard. Of course it would be lovely to be able to do a project like this with every child but that may not always be possible.

One child I did this project with was fascinated by superheroes; all of the photos he took were of his Batman and Spiderman toys that he carried everywhere and the photos around the school were of all the superhero lunch boxes and water bottles he could find. When his new teacher saw this she made various superhero displays and bought some Batman LEGO® for her classroom, in preparation for the September. She also made superhero number and writing resources for him to use in Year 1. She listened to his interests, she acknowledged that he needed additional support and by recognising his interests she found a way to help him in his transition, which was wonderful to see.

Ways to use a photo/video project

This is a project that would work for:

- children in nursery going to school
- children going from a childminder to nursery/school
- children starting at a nursery/childminder/school with photos taken at home either on a home visit or by asking the parents to do it with the children
- children going from class to class or from room to room in nursery or school.

Obviously if you are doing a project like this you need to obtain all the appropriate consent.

All about me books (children from birth)

A resource you can make for children as part of their transition is an 'all about me' booklet. I know nurseries that have these in their baby rooms and toddler rooms for each child and childminders who also have these. This resource could also be used for pre-school and Reception children. With a child who is old enough to understand you can involve them in making this, choosing the photos or taking the photos themselves.

Having a booklet with photos of the child, what they enjoy doing, photos from home – for example of significant people/pets/favourite toy, and so on – is a lovely way to help the child feel they belong; it is a great link to home and can act as a comfort. Settings have the booklets available for children to look at with their key person. I have also seen some settings hang them on low hooks so the children can reach them and look at them when they choose.

To do this you are reliant on getting parents to send in photos, but if you give clear guidance and explain why you want them, parents are often happy to do this. Often settings laminate the booklets, helping them to last longer. It does take up some time to put these together, but they are a lovely resource to have and a great way to support a child in their transition. They can also be used to move up with a child from room to room.

Questions for practice

When new children arrive to your setting, do you give them a staggered start, with shorter sessions before they do their full hours?

Do you provide the children as well as the parents with information about your setting?

What attention do you give to the micro-transitions? Do you prepare children for these, for example, extra warning, visual timetables and so on?

References

Brodie, K. (2018) *The Holistic Care and Development of Children from Birth to Three*. Abingdon: Routledge.

Bryce-Clegg, A. (2017) *Effective Transition into Year One*. London: Featherstone.

Ephgrave, A. (2017) *Year One in Action: A Month-by-Month Guide to Taking Early Years Pedagogy into KS1*. Abingdon: Routledge.

Grimmer, T. (2018) *School Readiness and the Characteristics of Effective Learning*. London: Jessica Kingsley Publishers.

O'Connor, A. (2017) *Understanding Transitions in the Early Years: Supporting Change through Attachment and Resilience*. Abingdon: Routledge.

Chapter 6

Children's Voice in Learning and Planning

There is an increased recognition of the importance of following children's interest in their learning. A large number of people have been influenced by the creative and child-led practice of early years settings in Reggio Emilia, a northern town in Italy. Their work embeds creativity and a recognition that children express themselves through 'a hundred different languages' (Edwards, Nandini and Forman 1998). The Reggio approach believes that every child is a unique, strong and competent learner. As educators, they see their role as listening to and understanding how each individual child is communicating and they see the role of an educator as being a co-learner alongside each child.

Following children's interests (children from birth)

In the UK a large number of early years practitioners have been inspired by Anna Ephgrave's books (2015, 2018) on child-led learning and planning in the moment. This way of working enables and encourages practitioners to listen, hear and follow children's interests. Anna describes how in her infant school you would not see any 'forward planning or focus activities' (Ephgrave 2015). Research and practice has shown us that by following children's interests and passions, as staff we are able to extend and scaffold their thinking. When the children are already enthused and passionate about something, then they want to discover and learn more and we can follow these interests and extend their learning. This way of working is possible across the age range.

Example from practice: St Martins Garden Primary School, Bath

At St Martins Garden Primary the Reception class is using 'in the moment' planning. One very cold morning I was in the Reception class. It was one of the first very cold days that winter; the children were outside and had discovered there was ice in various tubs in the gardens. A group of five boys worked together to collect the ice; the teacher provided a large builders' tray for them to put the ice into. The group spent time together investigating the ice. One boy shouted with delight to his friend, 'It goes back to water, it goes back to water, look!' The teacher talked about melting and freezing. The children then proceeded to experiment with carrying the ice, dropping the ice, stamping on the ice, watching how it melted and turned into slush. They also pretended they had made an ice rink (one had just opened for Christmas in our city and one boy had seen it). The language, mathematical and science learning, the social skills and physical skills that came out of this one small interaction with ice were just wonderful. The teacher could have responded by telling the children they could look but not touch or by leading them to a planned activity but thankfully, as an excellent and experienced practitioner, she was able to scaffold children's learning through moments of the children's interest. She followed their curiosity and delight and encouraged them in their exploration. By working in this way, staff find the children's learning is extended far more than they expected.

Big floor books planning (children 18 months and over)

Another way of involving children in planning is through using an idea from Claire Warden (1995); she has created the Talking and Thinking Floorbook Approach™. This approach enables you to work with a small group of children, gathering their ideas and thoughts. It is a tool which helps you to observe, plan and document with the children. To use it a practitioner has a small number of resources which could link with children's interests and together they look at these and plan what they could do using large pieces of paper to document their ideas. I once observed a childminder using this approach. The children were interested in foxes and the resources were a toy fox, a picture of woods they visit, sticks, a story book, string and a picture of chickens. From these the children and childminder made plans for that week to: visit the local farm to buy some eggs, make a picnic, play a hiding game in the woods, make a house for the foxes in the wood, play chicken and fox games and to make pictures of foxes and their homes.

I have seen this approach used in childminder settings, nurseries and children's centres. It works best with small groups of children. You can find out more about Claire Warden's approach and ideas on her website, Mindstretchers,[1] which includes online training and resources.

Child voice in documenting learning (children from birth)

We know it is good practice to document children's learning. It enables us to share their ideas, their learning and their journey with the children, with parents, with colleagues and for moderation. Within early years using learning journals has been common practice for many years. However these are often adult-made journals; they will almost always include photos and drawings but they are documents that the key worker has pulled together. Many nurseries are now also using an online version of this. I know of some settings that involve the children in adding to their learning journals. The key person regularly meets with the child; together they go through the journal and they talk about what the child would like to go in it and images they would like included or not. They often use the child's words around the choices they have made in this. This is a simple but very effective way of sharing with children the documenting you are doing and involving them in the process. It is possible to do this both on the online versions and paper copies.

Another way of involving children in documenting is through making books with them. The Reggio Emilia approach is very well known for having one of the biggest documentation libraries of its children's work and re-

---

1   www.mindstretchers.co.uk/index.html

search. It has been documenting children's learning since the 1940s. For 20 years this was a world travelling exhibition called The Hundred Languages of Children; [2] it is now based in the Loris Malaguzzi international centre. If you are able to see this exhibition it is an inspiring visit. As part of the way Reggio documents it makes books of the children's work, research and words. Children are involved in putting together these beautiful books. (The UK distributor for these is Sightlines Initiative.)[3]

I have worked with a few nurseries that have been inspired by the Reggio way of documenting and make their own very simple books. They take photos of the current interest/ project the children have been working on and the staff make these into simple books for the children, using the photos and the children's words. Children help the staff to think about what images they want in the books and what words they want to use to go with the photos. The books are then put into the book area for the children to look at and share with one another, their parents and visitors. There have been many times when I have visited these nurseries and the children have proudly shown me one of their books. The books are very simply made on computers, printed out and laminated.

---

2   www.thewonderoflearning.com/history/?lang=en_GB

3   www.sightlines-initiative.com/publisher/publisher-reg-children.html

Child voice in day-to-day activities (children from birth)

We can include children's views and interests throughout the day's activities and in any type of daily work with children. My eldest daughter teaches four-year-olds bouldering. As part of her lessons she uses games during the sessions, and she always asks the children to suggest games each week. Towards the end of the term they always ask for sleeping lions; we suspect this is because they are very tired at the end of term and really need some time of stillness.

Another way of listening to children in daily practice is by asking them questions about what they already know before you start teaching something new. One example of this is a teacher who was talking about Chinese New Year. As a class, she asked the children what they knew already. They had a discussion about what they knew and what they wanted to know and together they came up with a list for them all to find out about. This included: what are the animals in the Chinese New Year? Do the Chinese have a party at New Year? What clothes do they wear and what do they eat? Is it like Christmas? Do they go away for New Year? The teacher found there were questions she didn't know the answer to, so together the children and staff were able to find out. She also asked the children about where they could go to find out the information; one child suggested they visit the local Chinese takeaway.

Embedding children's choices and following children's interests is good practice throughout early years and is possible in pre-schools, nurseries, schools and with childminders. Below is an example of how some childminder friends of mine do this, in their own words.

Example from practice: Louie and Jim, childminders

This week we planned to go to the woods for some forest school experience. One of the children is very interested in *The Gruffalo* (Donaldson 1999) story and dinosaurs so we decided to take the Gruffalo story props and some dinosaurs and see if we could add the dinosaurs into the story. As we discussed the plan for the morning with the children over breakfast another child added her suggestions of toys we could take. She is very interested in 'My Little Ponies', unicorns and fairies. We talked about making up stories in the woods and making a fairy house/den which she was very excited about. We also had two younger non-verbal children, so we talked to them about our plans and asked them to find some toys they would like to take. One child chose to take her favourite book and the other chose a shape sorter he loves playing with. Once at the woods we incorporated all the items we had taken with us; we had an extended story time using story props – dinosaurs, fairies, ponies and unicorns – as well as reading the book. We hid the shapes from the shape sorter under leaves to find and then post, and the older children made triangles and squares out of sticks and we discussed/problem solved how we could make a circle with straight sticks. The circle was made of leaves instead of sticks as directed by the children. We also had a really good explore looking for footprints from animals or fairies.

Questions for practice

Do you know what your children are currently interested in?

How do you use these interests in your planning?

How do you find out what children already know, before you teach them something new?

References

Donaldson, J. (1999) *The Gruffalo*. London: Macmillan.

Edwards, C., Nandini, L. and Forman, G. (1998) *The Hundred Languages of Children: The Reggio Emilia Approach – Advanced Reflections*. London: Ablex Publishing.

Ephgrave, A. (2018) *Planning in the Moment with Young Children: A Practical Guide for Early Years Practitioners and Parents*. Abingdon: Routledge.

Ephgrave, A. (2015) *The Nursery Year in Action: Following Children's Interests through the Year*. Abingdon: Routledge.

Warden, C. (1995) *Talking and Thinking Floorbooks: An Approach to Consultation, Observation, Planning and Assessment in Children's Learning*. Crieff: Mindstretchers.

Chapter 7

Children's Voice in Redesigning Classroom and Outdoor Spaces

Involving children and listening to their ideas in the redesigning of classrooms and outdoor spaces is becoming an embedded practice for many early years settings. This has been largely influenced by the excellent work of Clark and Moss (2001) in the Mosaic approach. Thanks to Alison Clark and Peter Moss, early year practitioners from across the country have been using this approach to find out from children what they think of the nursery/classroom/ outdoor spaces and to be involved in changing them. It makes complete sense to me to involve children in this; it is their space and they spend a lot of time in it so they should have a say in any changes. It is so noticeable when children have been involved in this; I find the space often feels more child friendly. There is now a new edition of the Mosaic approach (2017) which expands on the authors' original ideas.

Mosaic approach (children from 18 months onwards)

This model is about finding out from children what they like/dislike in their nursery/classroom/outdoor play space. To use this model I would suggest reading the 2017 edition of Clark and Moss's book, as this will clearly talk you through the stages. As a brief summary I describe below how I have used it:

Practitioners should start by talking to the children about how they are going to make changes to the space and want to find out what the children think. Start with conversations and writing down the children's ideas and thoughts. Then give the children cameras and ask them to take photos. When I use this approach I often do it over a few sessions, asking the children to first take photos of what they like in the space. Then we come back together and look at the photos, talk about the photos: what they have taken and why. Write down these thoughts and ideas. Next (usually on another day) ask the children to take photos of what they would like to change, and come together to discuss them as before. The Mosaic approach books also talk about tracking what the children use and how they use it through completing observations and interviewing the children about their thoughts and ideas.

From this activity you will then have a wealth of information about what the children like and dislike about the space. You are then ready to think about how you change it. Of course as adults you will already have some thoughts about the possible changes; you will know your budget and the possibilities and constraints. Share these with the children, talk to them about the amount of money you have. Although this will be abstract for them, it is such an important start and lesson in helping them to begin to learn about money, prices and budgeting.

In the 2017 edition of *Listening to Young Children* Alison Clark suggests making the photos into a photo book; this provides a lovely form of documentation that the children and staff can revisit and use to help them in their planning.

You can then involve children in making decisions about buying new equipment, choosing colours and designs and where new items should go.

Using video (children aged two years and over)

As well as using photos you could ask children to video the nursery or setting. This enables you to see the space at their level, though their eyes. You can then look at the video together and talk about what you all see: what you like and dislike and what you would like to change.

Case example

At one children's centre in a coastal area, we were working on a listening to children project as part of their training. They wanted to make changes to their entrance as they felt it looked drab and uninviting. The entrance had a slope which children liked to race down. For one week staff met children as they arrived at the entrance to the centre, gave them a video camera and asked them to film their arrival. The children and parents were keen on this (parents had been informed in previous weeks about this project). Staff then watched the films with the children and parents; what they all saw were grey concrete walls and paving. The children, parents and staff said this was boring and unwelcoming. The staff worked with the children to find out what they would like on the entrance route. The children said they wanted pictures of the sea and sea animals. The staff contacted local businesses about their plans and they were given wood, paint and varnish as donations. Together staff worked with the children to make sea creature pictures, which each child attending was involved in designing and making. The slope down to the centre displayed these pictures, this very simple project transforming the entrance.

Drawing on maps (children age two years and over)

This activity can be used alongside the above examples or on its own. Some children love maps. For this activity make a map of your outdoor or indoor space and get the children to make marks on the map, drawing draw their ideas of how the room or space could be changed. For example they may draw large cushions in one area to lie on or they may draw a tented area to hide in. Have conversations with the children before and afterwards about this, about what they have added and why. This activity works best if it is out for a few days or a week so children can revisit it, react to it and add to it. Maps can also be used once you have decided what you are changing and purchasing and you can use small photos or objects for the children to place on the map to show you where they would like things to go.

Wishing net (children aged two years and over)

This idea is taken from Penny Lancaster's *Listening to Young Children* pack (2003). It can be used as part of planning a new area. Provide pens and cloud-shapes pieces of paper and a net. Ask the children to draw what their wishes are for the changed outdoor space/classroom. Once they have drawn them they need to add them to the net. Together with the children, look at their ideas and talk about the drawings and the changes they have suggested. (I also describe how this can be used in the assessment process in Chapter 9.)

Catalogues and pictures (children aged 18 months and over)

This idea can be used alongside taking photos and video. Once decisions have been made and you know what your budget is, you need to involve the children in spending the money. One very simple way to do this is by first talking to the children about the budget. This will be abstract but it is a good early lesson in budgeting. Then show pictures from either catalogues or photos you have taken of the choices for the new equipment, toys and so on.

One way to do this is by putting each photo/image on a separate piece of paper, then giving children stickers, either one or two, and asking them to put a sticker on the item they most want. You are using a very simple voting tool by doing this. This can be used for choosing any new equipment, colour swatches for re-painting, flowers and vegetables they can grow in the garden, new books to buy and so on.

Choosing plants (children aged one year and over)

Many settings involve children in choosing what plants to grow in their garden each year. This is a lovely way to involve children in growing food and plants from a young age; we know that children need to spend more time outside and be encouraged to learn about food we can grow and eat. I talk about this more in my book on children's wellbeing (Mainstone-Cotton 2017). If you are growing things with children, I would always recommend you involve them in choosing what you grow. You could talk about this as a group, perhaps tasting examples of different food you could grow and getting them to think about what they like and don't like. You can talk about how some plants need more room than others. If as a staff team you are a bit unsure about good plants to grow, ask parents if there any keen gardeners and invite them in to talk to the children about growing plants (you are almost certain to have one or two keen gardeners among your parents). You could get the children to choose from seed catalogues, or better still take a trip to a garden centre. While there look at the different plants, see them, smell them, touch them. Talk to the children about how much money you have and what that means, for example, 'We can buy ten packets of seed and two plants that cost £5 each.' You could get the children to ask the garden centre staff some questions about what you want to grow. It is great to involve children in the whole process, from the choosing, buying, planting, caring, picking and eating. There is so much learning of maths, science, language and physical development that you will cover in this.

Questions for practice

How have you involved children in changes to your outdoor space/classroom or in buying new toys?

Do you have a listening to children policy which states you will involve children in future changes to the design and development of your service?

References

Clark, A. (2017) *Listening to Young Children, Expanded Third Edition: A Guide to Understanding and Using the Mosaic Approach.* London: National Children's Bureau.

Clark, A. and Moss, P. (2001) *Listening to Young Children: The Mosaic Approach.* London: National Children's Bureau.

Lancaster, P. (2003) *Listening to Young Children: The Reader.* Buckingham: Open University Press.

Mainstone-Cotton, S. (2017) *Promoting Young Children's Emotional Health and Wellbeing.* London: Jessica Kingsley Publishers.

Chapter 8

Children's Voice in Community Spaces

When I was involved in participation work, the team I worked with regularly collaborated with parishes and local authorities to involve children in the redevelopment of community spaces. During the early 2000s this happened a lot, particularly when there was money available from the Labour government for play spaces and play equipment. Although there is far less money available today, areas are still being redeveloped all the time. In the city where I live there are currently two big new housing developments taking place. As part of this there will be new play areas and community spaces. Also housing associations often receive money to redevelop the play area and community spaces. It is worth being aware of any new developments in your area and finding out if your children can have an involvement.

It is very common for local authorities or parish councils to consult with children of seven and over but they often find it harder to consult with children under seven. As a team, we specialised in consulting with children across the ages in a way which was appropriate to their age and understanding. The key in this work is to enable all the children to have a voice. If there was a choice to be made about equipment for older and younger children, we would make sure the children of the relevant ages were consulted on this. This section will offer some ideas on how to do that.

Photo journeys (children aged 18 months and over)

One key way we listened to children in community spaces work was by organising photo journeys; this style of working was very much influenced by the Mosaic approach (Clark and Moss 2001). We always advised groups/areas to find out first what children liked and disliked in their area before making changes. If we were working in a village or local area we put up posters explaining who we were and that we were organising a photo journey. We also sent letters to local schools and nurseries. We would invite parents and children to meet with us at a set time and place. We would go on a photo journey together with children taking photos of what they liked and disliked.

We always ensured we had plenty of workers with us to be able to fully document what the children were saying and photos they were taking. Children would take photos of what was important to them. Sometimes this would be a swing or a slide they enjoyed; one child took a photo of underneath the slide and told us, 'I like it under here, it's my den.' Photos often included trees and flowers and also lots of dog poo and rubbish. We found that children frequently took photos of the ground. I remember one child taking a photo of the flooring in the park which had a square pattern with grass growing in each square. When asked, the child said they liked finding bugs in the gaps.

Once we collated all the photos we would then look at them with the children and talk about what they liked and wanted to keep; we also discussed what needed changing. From this, we were then able to start to plan for any changes.

The beauty of doing photo journeys is the way it enables the adults to see the environment through the child's eye. Each time I have done this activity with children, I have discovered things I didn't know about the environment, for example, the best place to find bugs, where all the rubbish gets blown to, how bumpy the underneath of a swing is and why children like that.

Practice example

In my village the parish council had some money to renew the play equipment. At first they planned to choose the equipment themselves, based on what they thought children wanted. I persuaded them to let me work with the children in the village. We did a photo journey with the village children, around the play area and fields. The children took photos of the broken swing, dog poo, litter on the ground. They also all took photos of the large slide. All the children loved the slide. The adults wanted to take the slide away as it was very high but through the work with the children we persuaded the adults to keep it. The children were also involved in choosing the new equipment, through looking at catalogues and by choosing with stickers.

Using images to make changes (children two years and over)

Once it has been agreed what changes are happening, for example funding for a new bench or new swing or whole new play area, and once you know what the children like and dislike about the current space, you then need to plan with the children what changes will happen. One easy way to do this is to show children images of the things that can be bought with your budget. Make sure you explain to the children what the budget is and how much it can buy, for example it could either buy one swing and one bench or one small climbing frame. You can use a catalogue to show children what they could get. When you're doing this ensure that you are only using images of products that you can afford to buy.

With some groups, we also took them to visit parks which had similar equipment to the ones they could buy. The children were able to try out and play on the equipment and think about whether it would work in their park or play area.

To enable children to make the choices we would use a sticker vote, each child getting a sticker to put on the photo of the of equipment they prefer. The item with the most stickers gets purchased. This is a very simple method but it enables children to see how everyone had a vote.

Designing play areas with plasticine (children aged three and over)

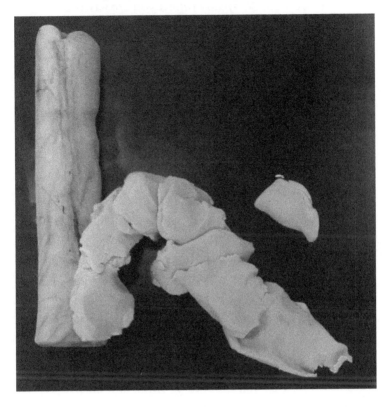

Ask the children what they would like in the new community play area. Talk about the things that could be there, then ask the children to make these with plasticine. Plasticine is very mouldable and works perfectly for this activity; you could also provide other scrap materials, for example pipe cleaners and straws. The big bonus of this activity is that you can do it anywhere and it is small scale; I have used it with children in parks, in church halls and in a nursery. Once the children have made their model, speak to each child about what they have made and write down their words and take photographs of the models. Include the words and images in any report you are writing.

Following through and feeding back

With this type of work, it is vital that the adults follow through on what the children have told them and feed back about how the project is progressing. We know that sometimes it can take a while from consulting children about changes to the changes actually happening. We need to explain the process to children in a way they will understand. For example, three-year-olds can understand that it will take a little while for the new park equipment to arrive; however you need to revisit this with the children by re-looking at the images of the equipment and talking about where it will go and how they will play on it. When I led on participation work I saw too often that children were asked their opinion but adults didn't get back to them to inform them what would happen next. We need to respect children when we ask them their views and ensure we are always feeding back to them.

Questions for practice

What links do you have with your local community?

Can you find out about any new developments in your area? If there are any contact your local councillor and ask if your children could be involved in this.

References

Clark, A. and Moss, P. (2001) *Listening to Young Children: The Mosaic Approach.* London: National Children's Bureau.

Chapter 9

Children's Voice in Assessment

As early years workers we will often be involved in assessments for children. It is essential that we hear the voice of the child through our assessment processes. Again we need to remind ourselves that it is easy for us as adults to presume we know how it is for a child, but we can never fully understand their world unless we stop and listen to them and view the world through their eyes. Eileen Munro (2011) was particularly vocal about this when she reviewed social services practice.

We have many different assessment processes for children, some examples of these are:

- the assessment used by early help assessment (previously called Common Assessment)

- assessment as part of social services

- assessment in the Education Health Care Plans

- assessment in the EYFS.

There have been ongoing concerns about the lack of involvement of younger children in the assessment process; this was a concern when I started working in participation in 2001. Back then Eileen Munro (2001) was calling for social services to empower looked after children to have a greater say in decision making made about them, the need for them to be involved in the assessment process and ongoing enablement to have a voice in decision making. She acknowledged this is a complex task but one we must tackle. In 2009 I co-wrote a piece about how we can hear young children's voices in the common assessment framework (Rose and Mainstone-Cotton 2009). The article came about due to concerns from our local authority about the number of CAFs that were being completed for children aged under seven, where the children were considered too young to give their views, according to the box for children's views on the form. This led to an authority-wide training programme where I and colleagues trained people in how to gather the views of your children for this process.

Now thankfully I rarely hear the phrase 'too young to give their view'. However I know there is still a lack of really hearing children's voices in the assessment process. I particularly see this through one page profiles which are sometimes used for children transitioning from nursery to school and often used in the Education Health Care plans, however I know this is also an issue in some social services assessments. The one page profiles are supposed to capture and include the child's views but in my experience they rarely do. For me a one page profile means so much more when it involves the child's actual words, not words interpreted by an adult. During a review meeting this week for one of my four-year-old nurture children who is a looked after child, the staff had been asked to gather his views for the meeting. One of the questions on the assessment form was what he would like to do when after leaving school; his answer was fly a drone. This was brilliant. It captured him – his imagination, his curiosity – in such a simple way.

The rest of this section is going to offer some simple ideas on how to capture the child's voice in the assessment process. (For more ideas specifically around hearing children's views in assessment Audrey Tait and Helen Wosu's book (2013) has a wealth of ideas and suggestions.)

Using images/video (children aged two and over)

I have talked about using photos in earlier parts of this book. The Mosaic approach (Clark and Moss 2001) tool can easily be used in the assessment process; I have seen this used really well for assessment by social workers, early years workers and teachers.

One way to use this is to ask the child to take photos of things that are important to them in their life. One social worker did this as part of a listening project on my training she attended; the four-year-old child took photos of her bedroom, her cat and her dolls. This enabled the social worker to be able to talk to the child about the things that were important to her and why and this information enhanced the assessment process and brought the child to life through the paperwork.

At one nursery I was supporting they were filling in a CAF for a two-and-a-half-year-old child who had no verbal communication. With the parents' permission they made a short video of the child, filming him doing things he loved, which was playing on a sit-on car and filling and emptying its 'boot' under the lift-up seat. This small piece of film showed him so well. It showed what he loved most at nursery but it was also clear from this seven-minute clip what he found hard and needed support with. I and the panel who saw this felt it really captured this little boy, enabling him to communicate in his own way and show us what was important to him.

Using photos of the setting (children aged two and over)

One simple way to find out what a child enjoys doing in school/nursery is to print off photos from the day, for example of carpet time/outside play/sandpit/toys/lunch time. Show these to the child and use a happy cut out face and a sad cut out face. Ask the child to put each photo on the happy face or the sad face. Ask the child about their choices and why they've made them; they may not be able to say why, but it is important to ask. Write down the actions of the child and any comments. This is best done with a key person who the child knows and trusts. The same activity could be used for a young child with photos from home by a social worker for a child protection assessment.

Using creative processes (children aged three and over)

Often children find it very hard to sit and talk to an adult about how things are for them and what is happening in their lives. Giving children opportunities to express this creatively can be very helpful. You can use drawing and painting, providing paper and pens or paint for the child to express themselves with. Ask the child a question, for example, 'I would like to know what makes you happy at school. Can you draw me a picture?' Ask the child about their drawing and write down their comments. Ask the child if you can photocopy the picture to include with the paperwork.

Plasticine (children aged three and over)

Plasticine is a great tool for children to model with; it works a lot better than play dough as it is more solid and mouldable. Ask children a question, for example, 'What would help you in school? Can you me make me something to show me?' Ask the child about the model and write down their comments. Take a photo and attach it to the paperwork.

Puppets (children aged three and over)

Some children are much happier to tell you their thoughts and feelings through a puppet. You can ask the child if they could tell the puppet something, for example, 'My puppet was wondering what is making you worried. Could you tell it?' Write down their comments, using their words and include these in the paperwork.

Alternatively the child could act out for you what they want you to know. I used this model with a group of young children in the care system. We wanted to make a film for social workers about what the children thought the social workers should know about being in the care system. The children decided to do a puppet show, and used the puppets to say how they felt, which was largely sad that they didn't get to see their mummy very often and cross that the social workers were too busy to listen to them. The latter was shown by the social worker being portrayed by a crocodile which kept saying 'I am too busy'. This film was shown in a local authority conference.

Using technology (children aged three and over)

Most children and young people love using technology and are brilliant at it. You can use this as a tool for children to share their views. You could video them, voice record them or use apps such as PuppetPals, an app that allows you to make a puppet show and record your voice. I have used this with children of varying abilities from the ages of three to 18 years.

Wishing net (children aged three and over)

This idea is taken from Penny Lancaster's *Listening to Young Children* pack (2003). For this activity provide pens, pieces of paper in the shape of clouds and a large net. Explain to the child you want to know their wishes for...and explain you are going to take their wishes with you to let other people know. Ask the child to draw (or write depending on their age) what they are wishing for. This might be their wishes in the next class, what they would wish to happen at home or what they wish to happen in nursery. Then put this into the wishing net; they can put as many wishes as they want into the net. Ask the child about what they have drawn and write down their words. Include the pictures and words in the assessment paperwork.

Questions for practice

When you are filling in one page profiles, do you use the child's words?

How are you creatively involving children in the assessment process? For adults looking at the paperwork, a child is really brought to life for them when they hear from the child directly through their words and drawings.

References

Clark, A. and Moss, P. (2001) *Listening to Young Children: The Mosaic Approach.* London: National Children's Bureau.

Lancaster, P. (2003) *Listening to Young Children: The Reader.* Buckingham: Open University Press.

Munro, E. (2001) Empowering looked after children. Accessed on 21/06/2018 at https://eprints.lse.ac.uk/357/1/Empowering_Looked_After_Children_2001.pdf

Mainstone-Cotton, S. and Rose, J. (2009) 'Hearing Young Children's Voices in the Common Assessment Framework.' *Every Child Journal 1*, 1.

Munro, E. (2011) The Munro review of child protection final report. Accessed on 15/12/17 at https://assets.publishing.service.gov.uk/government/uploads/system/uploads/attachment_data/file/175391/Munro-Review.pdf

Tait, A. and Wosu, H.(2013) *Direct Work with Vulnerable Young Children: Playful Activities and Strategies for Communication.* London: Jessica Kingsley Publishers.

Chapter 10

Children's Voice in Family Support

On the listening to young children course that I deliver, many of the staff work in children's centres and are family support workers. I believe there is a real challenge in the delivery of family support work; the challenge can be that the needs of the parents are so high that it is easy to lose sight of the child in the work. I have been a family support worker myself, and I know that sometimes when we arrive to work with a family, the parents are in crisis. At these times it is easy to spend the whole visit focusing on the parent and to barely notice the child. Through the training, we look at ways we can support the practitioners to help them remember to spend time focusing on the child. I often remind staff that they are employed to work with the whole family and this should include the child in the majority of visits. I also remind staff that if they are working with children in the family home, they need to use tools to enable them to hear the child's views

Keeping the child at the centre of family support work

Keeping children at the centre of family support is good safeguarding practice. As mentioned in Chapter 3, on the consequences when we don't listen to children, there have been too many times when the child has been overlooked. As mentioned above, it can be a real challenge to keep the child at the centre of any family support work. We know that the families we work with have enormous needs, and so often the needs of the parents can shadow what is happening to a child. We need to start work with families by stating right at the beginning that we are there to work with the child and parents. A straightforward way to do this is by sending a letter to the parents and then also sending a separate letter to the child. In this letter, I suggest you put a photo of the worker. Here is an example of a letter to a child:

Introductory letter to a child

Dear Lucy

My name is Sonia

I will be visiting you and Mummy next Monday. I am looking forward to seeing you both and finding out what you like to play with. I will bring some toys with me so we can do some playing and we will do some talking.

From

Sonia

By sending a letter to the child as well as the parent you are helping to keep the child at the centre of the work right at the beginning. You are reminding parents you are there to see both the child and parent and you are helping the child to be prepared for seeing you, a new person, entering their home. One team from a children's centre I recently worked with started to use this with all their new cases. One member of staff described how she arrived at a home for a first visit; the child was excited to see her, telling her, 'I got your letter, I have been waiting for you.'

Keeping the child at the centre of reports and visit notes

Another way to remind staff of the importance of keeping the child at the centre of the work is by having some child-related questions on your session visit notes. It can all too often be easy to forget to mention how the child was and be taken up by comments about the discussion you had with parents. Having questions on the paperwork helps to remind staff to keep the child at the centre of the work.

Example questions for paperwork

How was the child today?

How did they present?

What did the child tell you today?

What emotions did the child show you today?

Were there any safeguarding issues from today's visit?

By having these questions as part of your paperwork you are helping staff to remember to keep the children at the centre of the work. You can then use these in supervision sessions, again helping to keep the focus on the child.

Some family support teams also write their actions plans with the child at the centre. See the following for an example:

Example of an action plan

Lucy needs Mummy to take her medication every day to keep her well.

Lucy needs her bedroom to feel warm and safe:

Mummy and Daddy will decorate Lucy's new room with help from...charity.

Daddy and Mummy will put a rug in her bedroom.

Mummy and Daddy will put curtains in her window.

Lucy says she would like to have yellow walls and a red rug. This will be done by...

Lucy, Mummy and Daddy will meet with Sarah the family support worker each week for one month to play and talk.

All about me cards

When we start working with a family, a child, there are often lots of questions we have and information we need to find out about the family. This can be quite intimidating for families and children. In my old team we created some 'all about me' cards; these are small, pictorial information cards, on a key fob. Each team member had them. When we met a new child or family that we were working with, we used these cards to tell them something about ourselves. The cards have both pictures and words. You only put information on the cards that you are happy to share with the family. The information on my cards is below:

All about me cards

I am Sonia and my job is to listen to and work with children (photo of me).

Things that I like (photos of my family, chocolate, swimming and the outdoors).

Things I don't like (photos of mice and a view from a height).

My hopes and dreams: learn to play the cello, visit New Zealand, see whales in the wild (photos of all of these).

Recognising the family's emotions and feelings at the beginning of the work

It is important to help families to use language about their emotions and have a good emotional understanding. In my book promoting young children's emotional health and wellbeing (Mainstone-Cotton 2017) I talk about how vital it is that we use emotion language with children; we can share this with parents by directly modelling this through the words we use, sharing scripts with parents that they can use and by talking about feelings and emotions. It is not unusual to find that in many of the families we work with the parents have low emotional literacy. The intentional use of an emotional vocabulary in our work is good for both the children and as a model to parents.

At the start of each session with a family, you can use emotion images and talk about how you are all feeling; get everyone to take it in turns to look at the images and say how they are feeling today. With children under the age of five use just a few images, for example happy, sad, tired, cross. You can make your emotion pictures using either photos or cartoon faces. There are also some good resources you can buy, for example emotion cards, books, dice and emotion stress balls. I always recommend that the worker takes part in this too; by taking part you are able to model to the parents and child the importance of recognising how you feel. By doing emotion work at the beginning of the session, you are intentionally starting the session by listening to the child and recognising how they are feeling in that moment; you can then respond appropriately to the child's feelings. Recognising the child's feelings at the beginning of the session is useful for both you as a worker and for the parents to hear and see.

Scripts we can share with parents

My colleagues and I use scripts all the time as nurture workers. They are an excellent way to validate and recognise how a child is feeling. We share the scripts we use in schools with the parents, so they can use them at home as well. Here are some scripts I use regularly:

I can see you are feeling…but it is not ok to…I am here to help you feel safe.

I can see and hear that you are feeling very cross that I said no. I care how you feel, but I am still saying no.

I am here for you.

I can feel that you are very sad. I am here for you.

Family support bags

The listening to young children training I deliver is a one-and-a-half-day training delivered with a six-week gap. Over the six weeks, the participants need to work on a listening project. Quite a few groups have made family support bags as part of this project, which are intended to be a toolkit in family support sessions. These are individual bags for each family support worker and each bag will be unique to the worker.

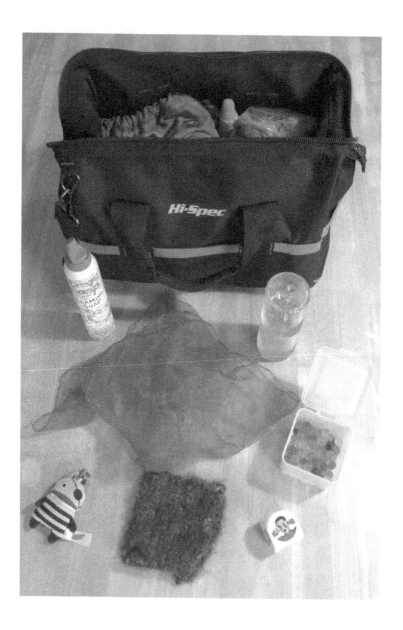

The items I have in my bag are:

Emotion cards

Play dough or plasticine

Bubbles

Stickers

Small tin of LEGO® or DUPLO® (depending on age)

Sand timer

Hand cream

Natural play things, e.g. shells, pine cones

Tin of buttons

Scarves/material

Finger puppets

Paper

Pens/crayons

Books

Sensory rice (rice painted/dyed and scented with lavender oil; see Pinterest[1])

A small game, e.g. snap or dominoes

Lavender pillow (knitted or sewn with lavender seeds inside)

A fiddle toy, e.g. tangle or stretchy man

---

1   https://theimaginationtree.com/natural-lavender-sensory-rice/

An emotion stress ball

Pictorial cards with the words and images of writing/playing/talking.

The aim of the kit is to have tools to engage the children during the session and tools to help with listening to them. This bag works with children and young people across the ages. I get the children to look through the bag and choose what they want to play with and explore. Sometimes parents also find something they want to explore, for example the fidget toy. At the beginning of the session I use the pictorial cards and explain to the child that we need to do some talking, writing and playing. I get the child to choose the order we do it in. This is again a very simple of way of keeping the child at the centre of the work and ensuring they make some decisions for the session.

I also suggest that workers have some pictures in the bag of toys or activities they could bring for the next session and get the child to choose what they would like to do, for example a picture of going to the park, a game or messy play. Make sure you only have images of things that you can take in and that the parents are happy for you to do. Also if I have a child with a particular interest I will try to include that in the bag, for example for a child who likes dinosaurs or My Little Pony.

These bags do not need to be expensive to pull together. Staff who have put these together have fed back how useful they have been, how much the children love them and how it helped the workers to keep children at the centre of their work. It works best when staff make their own individual bags, putting things in that they really like; for example, if you really dislike play dough, there is no point in having it in your bag.

I also know social workers who have developed these packs and are using them in their daily practice. I recently read an inspiring book by Audrey Tait and Helen Wosu (2013) and they describe a similar bag that they have in their car to use on all visits with children. Using these tool bags really helps us to listen to children; they are far more likely to tell us things and explore their feelings when they have tools to help them.

Questions for practice

How do you keep children at the centre of your work?

Do you review regularly to check that you are keeping children at the centre of your work?

References

Mainstone-Cotton, S. (2017) *Promoting Young Children's Emotional Health and Wellbeing.* London: Jessica Kingsley Publishers.

Tait, A. and Wosu, H. (2013) *Direct Work with Vulnerable Children: Playful Activities and Strategies for Communication.* London: Jessica Kingsley Publishers.

Conclusion

Throughout this book I have shared ideas and suggestions for how to embed a culture of listening to children in your daily work. For me the joy of listening to and working with children is that you never quite know what will happen and what they will tell you. I have learnt so much from the children I have worked with over the years.

The ideas in this book are just the starting point but hopefully they will inspire you and help you to think creatively about ways in which you listen to children and ways in which you involve them in decision making.

I hope you have fun trying out some of these ideas.

Subject Index

Author Index